Moment for Morricone

for Saxophone Quartet

Music from "The Good, the Bad and the Ugly"
and "Once upon a time in the West"

E. Morricone

Score

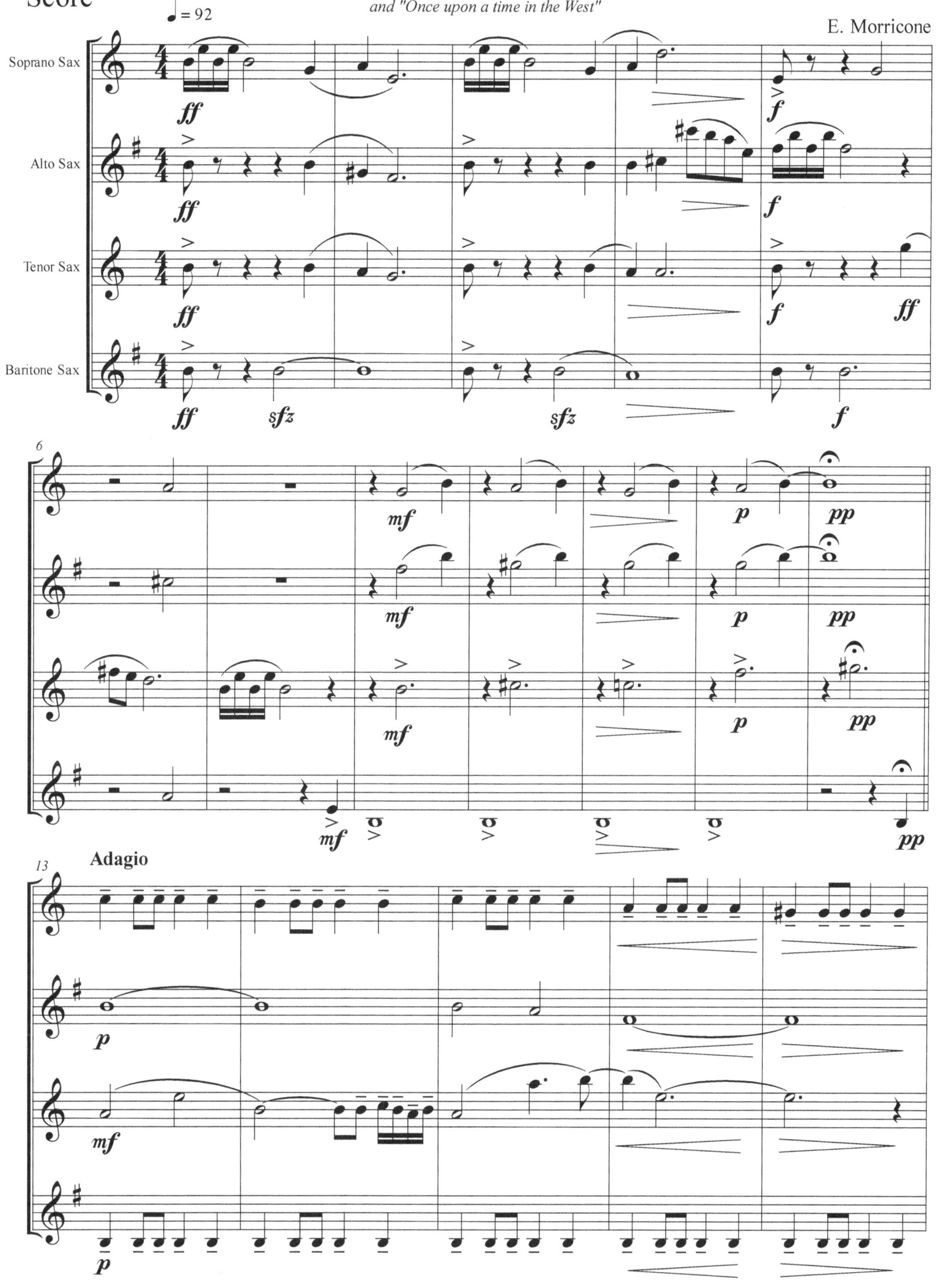

Più mosso

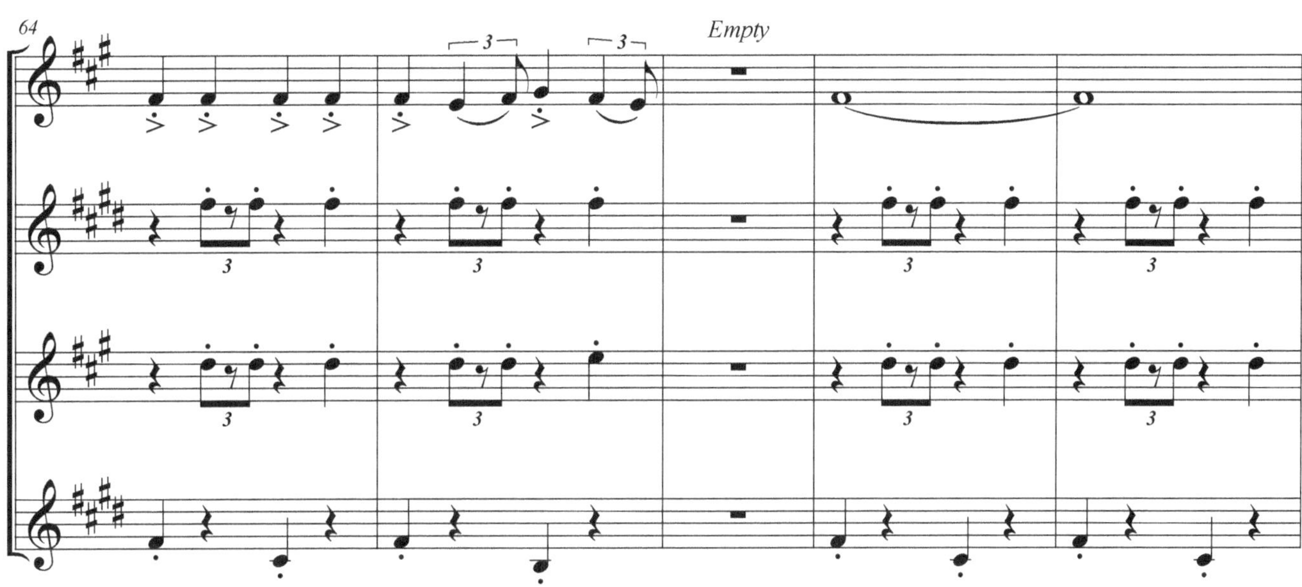
Empty

Più mosso
f
f
f
95
Allegro
101
f
f
f
f
f
f
f

rit.

Grandioso
f
f
ff
f

140
p f
p f
p f
p f
144 Vivace
p
p
p
p
147
p ff
p ff
p ff
p ff

Moment for Morricone

for Saxophone Quartet

Music from "The Good, the Bad and the Ugly"
and "Once upon a time in the West"

E. Morricone

Soprano Sax

Moment for Morricone

for Saxophone Quartet
*Music from "The Good, the Bad and the Ugly"
and "Once upon a time in the West"*

E. Morricone

Alto Sax

Moment for Morricone

for Saxophone Quartet

Music from "The Good, the Bad and the Ugly"
and "Once upon a time in the West"

Tenor Sax

E. Morricone

Moment for Morricone

for Saxophone Quartet

Music from "The Good, the Bad and the Ugly"
and "Once upon a time in the West"

E. Morricone

Baritone Sax

www.ingramcontent.com/pod-product-compliance
Lightning Source LLC
Chambersburg PA
CBHW060622120726
48002CB00010B/3072